D1717112

Shark Dentists

and other stories

VINCENT IMMORDINO

Illustrated by DAYNE SISLEN

Dedication

To my grandchildren and
great-grandchildren whom I love dearly

To my fifth grade teacher Mrs. Jolson,
who took an interest in me and changed my life

And to my Creator,
who plans all my days.

Acknowledgments

I would like to thank Stephanie Krell for her
part in bringing this book to life.

Shark Dentists
and Other Stories

Vincent Immordino

Text copyright © 2017 by Intelligent Design Press, Ltd.
Illustration copyright © 2017 by Dayne Sislen
Edited by Stephanie Krell

Library of Congress Control Number: 2017952813
ISBN 978-0-9993322-0-7

Intelligent
Design Press, LTD.

www.intelligentdesignpress.com

CHAPTERS

1. SHARK DENTISTS

Perhaps you have visited the dentist to have your teeth cleaned. Did you know that sharks also make trips to their dentists in order to take care of their teeth?

Yes, sharks!

Those *big* monsters with those *big* teeth in those *big* jaws. It's probably hard to imagine who would want to clean the teeth of these scary animals!

I am the remora fish, and I am happy to do it. Some of my cleaner fish friends and I take care of this very important task.

Sharks visit fish dentists like me at underwater cleaning stations. Cleaning stations are where underwater animals come to be tidied up by smaller creatures. My friends and I wait at the cleaning stations just to do the sharks' dental work!

When a shark is ready for its cleaning, it opens its mouth, shows its deadly sharp teeth and waits. This invites my friends and me to swim into its mouth. The food that is left between its teeth feeds us and we leave it with sparkly teeth.

Most people would likely say, "Legs, legs, do your stuff and get going fast!" when its mouth opens.

Not us!

We casually swim right in and get to work. You may think we're nuts for being so bold!

We have a deal with the sharks. We can eat all the bits and pieces of food we can get from their mouths. These scary fish will patiently sit there and enjoy the cleaning until we are finished because what we do helps them to stay healthy.

But how did this agreement between the sharks and cleaner fish come to be? Maybe a long, long time ago, sharks called a meeting with my relatives and asked them to come to help them out?

I don't think so!

Perhaps a friendly shark had its mouth open and a really brave remora swam up to clean his teeth.

Not a chance!

*The answer
is that God created the
sharks knowing they would need
help caring for their teeth, so He
created cleaner fish like me to be their
dentists. He made the whole world and
all living things in the beginning.
It was all part of the wonderful
plan of God.*

2. TERRANCE THE FRIENDLY

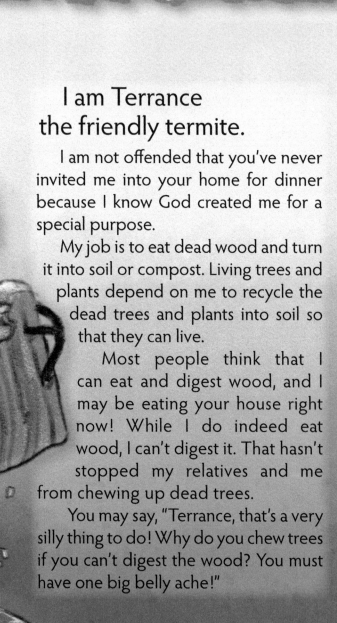

I am Terrance
the friendly termite.

I am not offended that you've never invited me into your home for dinner because I know God created me for a special purpose.

My job is to eat dead wood and turn it into soil or compost. Living trees and plants depend on me to recycle the dead trees and plants into soil so that they can live.

Most people think that I can eat and digest wood, and I may be eating your house right now! While I do indeed eat wood, I can't digest it. That hasn't stopped my relatives and me from chewing up dead trees.

You may say, "Terrance, that's a very silly thing to do! Why do you chew trees if you can't digest the wood? You must have one big belly ache!"

TERMITE

This chart shows the flagellates in my stomach

No, I feel very well, thank you!

You see, in my stomach lives a teeny, tiny animal called a flagellate. While my termite relatives and I need air to live, Freddie the flagellate would die in the presence of air. The only place he can live is in my stomach.

Freddie can't chew wood, but he can digest it. I chew the wood first and then he turns it into soil, giving us both the nourishment we need to live in the process. I would starve without Freddie, and he without me. While we would both die living apart, we work very well together doing what God created us to do.

Charles Darwin wrote about a story called Evolution. It says that animals only appeared millions of years after plants had already been on earth.

How could that be?

While I was not there when the world began, my great-great-great-grandparents many times over must have been. Otherwise, who would have recycled the dead trees into soil? If we hadn't been there, the floors of forests would have been covered with dead trees from over the years. Seeds from fruit, vegetables and trees wouldn't have the soil we make to help them live and grow.

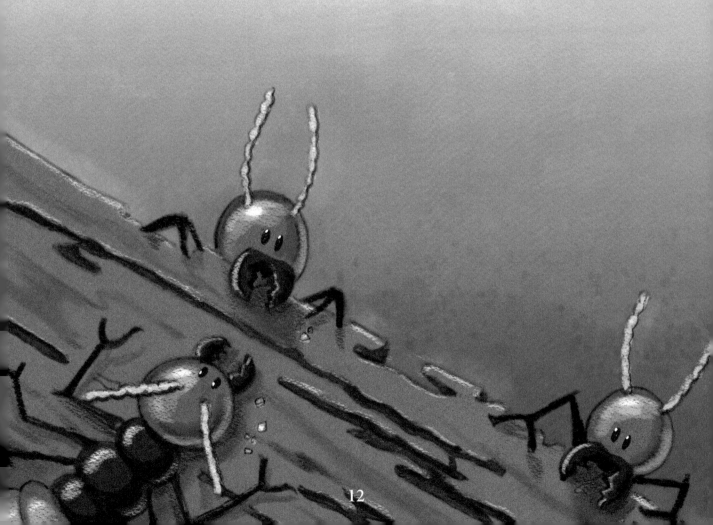

*There is only
one explanation for
how we got here. God
created Terrance the termite,
Freddie the flagellate, the
heavens, the earth, and
all living things
in six days.*

3. ANTS IN YOUR PLANTS

Hi. I'm a little old ant.

Your mother probably thinks my purpose in life is to drive her crazy by sneaking into your house! I'm actually a bigger part of God's great plan than it may seem.

I am a hard worker, and one of my jobs is gardening. One particular plant I like to work with is the wild violet. I help to spread and plant its seeds, and let me assure you, this is no simple task!

You might wonder why I take the trouble to do this. The reason is because the plant helps me too!

There is a part of the seeds which feeds both me and my babies. To me, it tastes like the best ice cream you've ever eaten! I can't resist the taste. But to get the seeds, I have to harvest them from the plant. Then I bring the seeds back to my nest. I remove the part of the seeds we can eat at my nest, and then I move the rest of it outside because I like to keep a clean house! The seeds then have a chance to grow where I have left them.

How does this help the plant?

Well, because I spread its seeds, the seeds have a better chance of surviving since they are not all trying to grow in the same place. Moving the seeds also protects them from animals who want to eat them, because sometimes these animals don't want to leave many behind to grow into new plants.

So you see, the wild violets and I make a good team! Their seeds help feed me, and I help the plants to reproduce and make new plants.

Some scientists say that plants were here for millions of years before the ants, and that eventually they learned to work together. But where did ants get the skills and knowledge to be gardeners in the first place? They can't even read!

*It only makes
sense that God gave
us ants the knowledge and
ability to garden plants. He
made the ants and plants,
along with the entire world
and all it contains over
a six-day period.*

4. CELIA THE CELL

Hello there!
I'm Celia the cell.

I am the smallest living part of all living things, and this includes plants, animals…even you! I am so little that you would need a special microscope that makes very tiny things look bigger just to see me.

Do you wonder what I am like?
I'll tell you!

All around my sides I have holes which open and close to take in the food and oxygen I need. These holes also get rid of garbage, just like how your family throws out the trash.

Inside of me is even more complicated! Just as a home often has a variety of rooms used for different purposes, I have various room-like sections where different jobs are done. All these jobs work together to keep me alive.

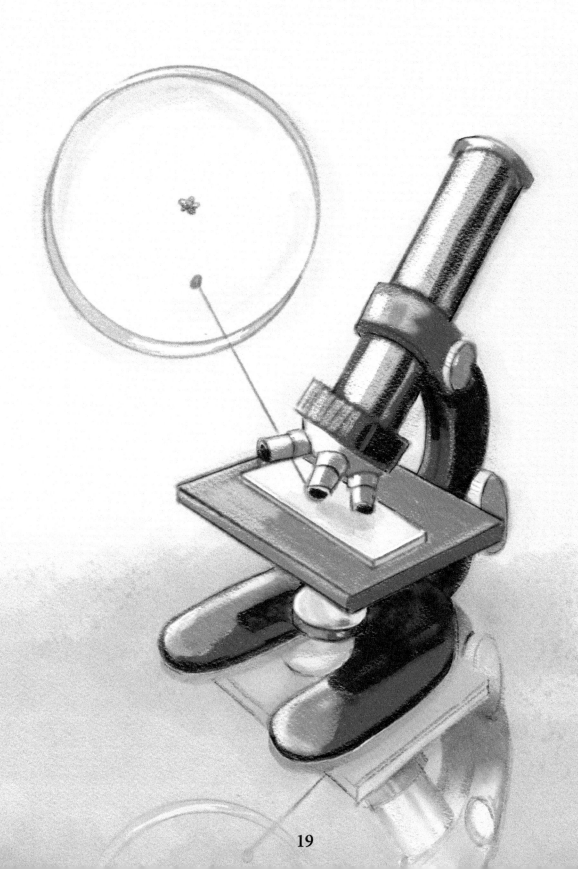

I also come with a full set of instructions, so that I know exactly what I am to do all on my own. Nothing is left to guessing.

Some people say I am just an accident, and that nobody designed me. If you told someone that no one made a watch, a car, or an airplane, they would probably think you were crazy! How could nobody have made me if I am much more complex?

I know the
only way I could
have been created is
by an amazing God who
designed the heavens,the
earth and all living
things at the begin-
ning of time.

5. UNIQUE YOU

Hi, I'm Molly the monkey.

A number of scientists say I am related to you because of something called Evolution.

What is Evolution?

It's a story about how living things in nature change over time and become new kinds of living things. One question it tries to explain is how humans came to be. It says that over many, many years, monkeys eventually became humans.

Why do many scientists believe this?

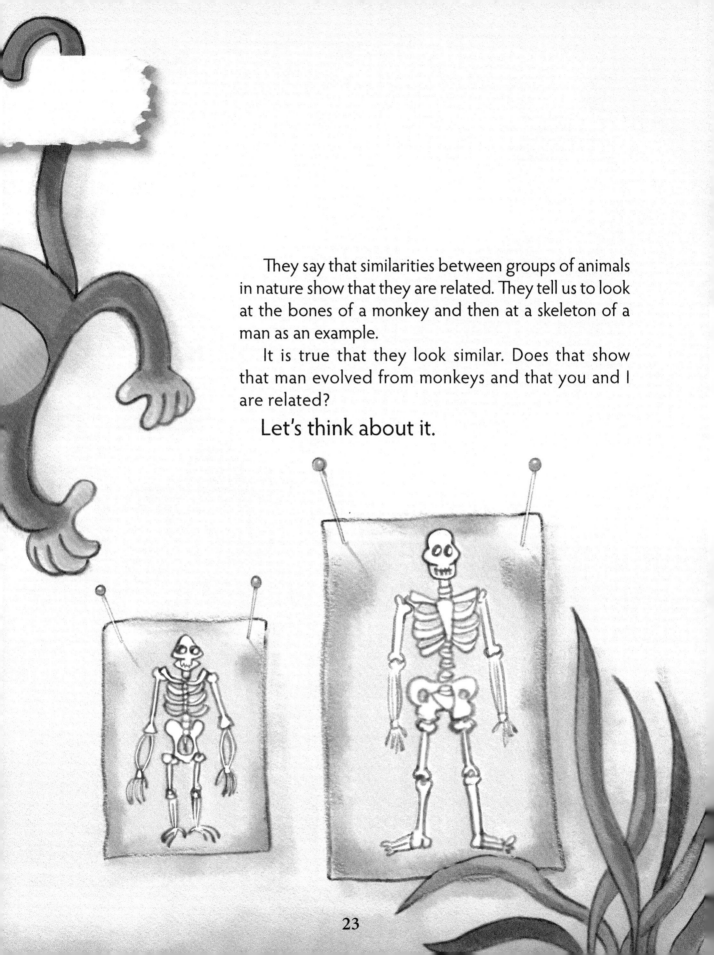

They say that similarities between groups of animals in nature show that they are related. They tell us to look at the bones of a monkey and then at a skeleton of a man as an example.

It is true that they look similar. Does that show that man evolved from monkeys and that you and I are related?

Let's think about it.

Single-family homes are similar to three-family homes. If you look in both, you'll find bathrooms, kitchens and bedrooms. Does that prove that a single-family home can grow into a three-family home?

Don't be silly!

The similarity of rooms in different-sized homes doesn't mean that one came from the other. It means that a common plan was used for both.

My monkey skeleton and a man's skeleton may have parts that look alike, but that doesn't mean that my monkey body could evolve into a man. All it proves is that our bodies were put together with a similar basic design.

Even though I've certainly seen children acting like monkeys, the only real relationship we have is that the same God made us both.

My friends and I say it is more believable that God created Molly and friends, all living things, the heavens and the earth in the beginning.

25

*The Bible
says God made
people on the final day
of creation. You are His
best and most unique
design of all!*

THINGS TO THINK ABOUT

I. Shark Dentists

1. Where do sharks go to get their teeth cleaned?

2. How does cleaning the sharks' teeth help the remora fish?

3. How did sharks and cleaner fish learn to work together?

Verse: So God created the great creatures of the sea and every living thing with which the water teems and that moves about in it, according to their kinds, and every winged bird according to its kind. And God saw that it was good. God blessed them and said, "Be fruitful and increase in number and fill the water in the seas, and let the birds increase on the earth." And there was evening, and there was morning—the fifth day.
Genesis 1:21-23

II. Terrance The Friendly Termite

1. What do living trees and plants depend on Terrance to do with the dead trees and plants?

2. Who helps Terrance turn dead trees into soil?

3. Why do forests need Terrance and Freddie to recycle the dead trees and plants in them?

Verse: He made the earth by his power;

he founded the world by his wisdom

and stretched out the heavens by his understanding.
Jeremiah 51:15

III. Ants In Your Plants

1. Why does the ant bring wild violet seeds to its nest?

2. Where does the ant put the seeds when it is finished with them?

3. Does the ant make it easier or harder for the seeds to grow into new plants by moving them?

Verse: Go to the ant, you sluggard;

consider its ways and be wise!

It has no commander,

no overseer or ruler,

yet it stores its provisions in summer

and gathers its food at harvest.

Proverbs 6:6-8

IV. Celia The Cell

1. Where are cells found?

2. What do the many jobs done inside of Celia the cell help her to do?

3. Is Celia the cell alive because of an accident, or did someone design her?

Verse: How many are your works, Lord!

In wisdom you made them all;

the earth is full of your creatures.

Psalm 104: 24

V. Unique You

1. What is the story called which talks about how living things in nature change over time and become new kinds of living things?

2. Evolution says that over a long period of time, monkeys eventually became what?

3. Do the similarities between the parts of a monkey and human body prove that they are related or that they were made by the same Creator?

4. What is God's most unique creation of all?

Verse: For you created my inmost being;

you knit me together in my mother's womb.

I praise you because I am fearfully and wonderfully made;

your works are wonderful,

I know that full well.

Psalm 139:13-14

PARENT REFERENCES

Chapter 1 (Sharks):

Genesis. NIV Study Bible. 3rd Version. Grand Rapids: Zondervan, 2002. Print.

Messenger, Stephen. "How One Genius Little Fish Convinces Sharks Not To Eat Them." *The Dodo.* Group Nine Media, 14 Aug. 2014. Web. 22 May 2017.

Earth Touch News. "Say 'ah!' Shark Lets Tiny Fish Clean Its Teeth." *Earth Touch News Network.* Earth Touch, 21 Apr. 2016. Web. 22 May 2017.

"Cleaning Station." *Wikipedia.* Wikimedia Foundation, 14 May 2017. Web. 22 May 2017.

Gill, Victoria. "Earth News - Hygienic Sharks Go to Cleaner Stations." *BBC.* BBC, 18 Mar. 2011. Web. 22 May 2017.

Chapter 2 (Termites):

First Land Plants and Fungi Changed Earth's Climate, Paving the Way for Explosive Evolution of Land Animals, New Gene Study Suggests." *Penn State Science.* Penn State Eberly College of Science, 09 Aug. 2001. Web. 22 May 2017.

Krishna, Kumar. "Termite." *Encyclopædia* Britannica. Encyclopædia Britannica, Inc., 30 Mar. 2017. Web. 22 May 2017.

Rozatoru, Michael. "Termite Extermination FOR BEGINNERS." The Evolution of Termite and Flagellate Mutualism: Answering The Question "Which Came First?" Termite Extermination For Beginners, 14 May 2011. Web. 22 May 2017.

Marshall, Michael. "Timeline: The Evolution of Life." *New Scientist.* New Scientist, 14 July 2009. Web. 22 May 2017.

Chapter 3 (Ants):

Ross, Erin. "Who Invented Agriculture First? It Sure Wasn't Humans." *NPR.* NPR, 25 Nov. 2016. Web. 19 May 2017.

Klein, Alice. "Fijian Ants Grow Their Own Plant Cities and Farm Tropical Fruits." *New Scientist.* New Scientist, 21 Nov. 2016. Web. 22 May 2017.

"Myrmecochory." *Wikipedia.* Wikimedia Foundation, 04 May 2017. Web. 18 May 2017.

Baskin, Carol C., and Jerry M. Baskin. "Chapter 10/G. Special Factor: Myrmecochery." *Seeds: Ecology, Bio-geography, and Evolution of Dormancy and Germination. Amsterdam*: Elsevier, 2014. Print.

"Seed Dispersal." *Australian Museum*. Australian Museum, 6 Oct. 2009. Web. 22 May 2017.

Chapter 4 (Celia):

Anderson, J. Kerby. "Chapter 7/Intelligent Design In Biology." *A Biblical Point of View on Intelligent Design*. Eugene, OR: Harvest House, 2008. 79-80. Print.

Iyer, Shyamala. "Building Blocks Of Life." ASU - *Ask A Biologist*. ASU - Ask A Biologist, 27 Sept. 2009. Web. 19 May 2017.

Cooper, Geoffrey M. "The Molecular Composition of Cells." *The Cell: A Molecular Approach*. 2nd edition. Sunderland: Sinauer Associates, 2000. *The National Center for Biotechnology Information,* https://www.ncbi.nlm.nih.gov/books/NBK9879/

Studios, Andrew Rader. "Cell Membranes." *Biology4Kids.com: Cell Structure: Cell Membranes.* Andrew Rader Studios, 23 Sept. 2014. Web. 13 May 2017.

"Cells as Building Blocks." Kids Discover: *Cells as Building Blocks. Kids Discover*, 6 Feb. 2012. Web. 22 May 2017.

Chapter 5 (Unique You):

Menton, Dr. David. "Did Humans Really Evolve from Apelike Creatures?" *Answers in Genesis.* Answers in Genesis, 25 Feb. 2010. Web. 19 May 2017.

Dunsworth, Holly. "Monkeys All The Way Down." *SAPIENS: Anthropology/Everything Human.* Wenner-Gren Foundation for Anthropological Research, Inc, 28 Jan. 2016. Web. 22 May 2017.

"History of Evolutionary Thought." *Wikipedia*. Wikimedia Foundation, 20 May 2017. Web. 22 May 2017.

"Evolution." *Merriam-Webster.* Merriam-Webster, n.d. Web. 9 April 2017.

Studios, Andrew Rader. "Read The Whole Page First." *Biology4Kids.com: Evolution.* Andrew Rader Studios, n.d. Web. 22 May 2017.

ABOUT THE AUTHOR

Vincent Immordino is the son of Sicilian immigrants. He served in the Navy on a submarine at the end of World War II and later worked for the New York Fire Department. He also spent many years as a public speaker and financial consultant. He enjoys extensive reading about politics, science and faith.

Mr. Immordino has made it his life's work to communicate why the Genesis Creation account is the most reasonable explanation for all that is around us. He resides in Queens, NY with his wife.

CPSIA information can be obtained
at www.ICGtesting.com
Printed in the USA
LVOW06*0018241117
557347LV00016B/180/P